HOMELESS TO HALL OF FAME

May God Bless You Always.

HOMELESS TO HALL OF FAME

Capt. Shane Watson

LIFE SENTENCE
—Publishing, LLC—

Visit Shane's website: www.lakelanierstripers.com

Homeless to Hall of Fame – Shane Watson

Printed in the United States of America

First edition published 2013

LIFE SENTENCE Publishing books are available at discounted prices for ministries and other outreach. Find out more by contacting info@lifesentencepublishing.com

LIFE SENTENCE Publishing and its logo are trademarks of

LIFE SENTENCE Publishing, LLC
P.O. Box 652
Abbotsford, WI 54405

Paperback ISBN: 978-1-62245-131-9

Ebook ISBN: 978-1-62245-132-6

10 9 8 7 6 5 4 3 2 1

This book is available from www.lifesentencepublishing.com, www.amazon.com, Barnes & Noble, and your local Christian bookstore.

Cover Design: Amber Burger

Editor: Mary Vesperman, Sheila Wilkinson

Share this book on Facebook:

Dedication

I dedicate this book to all the children of divorce, both young and old, who are searching for meaning and peace in their lives. I want to give them hope. After forty years of searching, I have come to a peace in my own life. I now realize that God loves me, and while there were times when I didn't realize it, he was watching over me and leading me, even when I didn't know he was there. My message to all the children out there is: God loves you. He is protecting you and watching out for you. He has a will and purpose for your life. He will show you the way. No matter how bad things seem right now, keep breathing and keep believing. Even though your earthly mother or father may have let you down, your heavenly Father will not.

I hope that my lifetime of loss and searching will help you in your life's walk and that by reading my story, you will find yourself and gain strength in our heavenly Father. I wish I could have learned the lesson of Isaiah 41:10 when I was a child. It would have helped me through some very dark times. I ask you to please look up and read this verse every day of your life and believe it always.

Contents

—⁓—

CHAPTER 1

My Early Story

———————————⟨∽⟩———————————

I was born in the 1960s into a seemingly normal, southern, middle-class family. My mother was an ambitious over-achiever who came from a sharecropper, farming family. Her dad was an outspoken kind of guy. He was a farmer and an avid outdoorsman. Her mother, my grandmother, was a saint.

My dad came from a somewhat affluent, local family, where my grandfather had a poultry farm and was a homebuilder. Both of my parents came from your classic, hardworking, WWII families – families with solid values, deep roots, and strong religious backgrounds. Both sets of my grandparents were great, dependable people who worked hard and provided great, stable, home lives for their children.

My mother and dad met when they were both young. My mother was in high school when they met. As many people in the fifties and sixties commonly did, they were married way too young. My mother was seventeen, and my dad was twenty. As an adult with teenage children of my own now, it makes me wonder, *what were they thinking? What were their parents and grandparents thinking?* I have been told that my mother's dad was quoted as saying to my mother, "Do not marry him; you will be throwing your life away." Well, my mother didn't listen and they were married.

They moved a time or two and then lived next to my grandmother in our small northern Georgia town, a town where everyone knew everyone and most people had lived there for generations. My dad commuted to Atlanta daily to his job, and my mother worked at a local bank and grocery store. Nine months after they were married, my brother was born. Four years later, I arrived. We had what seemed to be a perfect life. I can remember being as young as two years old and living next to my grandmother's house. My mother's dad died the same month I was born, and I was named after him and so was my second child. I sometimes wonder how our lives would have turned out if my grandpa had lived.

When I was little, I had a great life. My mother and

dad were great, and we had a normal family unit like every child deserves. I have great memories of going to Florida on vacations and going to my grandparents' house to play. Growing up in the sixties and seventies meant Saturday morning cartoons, Kool-Aid, hide-n-go-seek, and freeze tag. My grandmother next door watched children while their parents worked, so there was always somebody to play with. My brother was great; he was creative and always kept me entertained as he came up with new ways to play with our Hot Wheels and GI Joes.

My mother was wonderful when I was small. She was attentive, kind, protective, and fun. My dad was also very good to me when I was a small child. He would play with my brother and me and spend time with us when he wasn't working. They both loved us, and everything was perfect in my life until I was about four years old. That's when everything started to unravel. That was the last time in my life when I felt like I had a family.

It all started with my parents arguing and fighting all of the time. I can remember thinking, *what is going on? Why is this happening? What has happened to my family?* Things would get bad, and then things would get better for a while. I never knew what each day would bring.

During all of this up-and-down living, my mother accepted a job at a local real estate office, and we moved from next door to my grandmother's to a house on Lake Lanier. This was only a temporary move, and we later moved to another house on the lake. Everything seemed to be on track then. My folks were getting along, and we lived in a bigger house, which meant more room to play. Oh, I have some great memories of riding my big wheel down that driveway.

Our lives, however, were changing, whether we knew it or not. My mother's new career meant they were always inviting people over and were hosting and attending parties for one reason or another. Their parties remind me of wine bottles with candle wax melted down the sides of the bottle, and fondue. I guess those were seventies' things as my parents would keep putting a new and different-colored candle in the wine bottle whenever they had a party.

Being a child and living at the lake meant that I could go on boat rides and visit the houses of my mother's friends. It was fun, and I had a great life; things could not have been better – or so I thought. You may at this point think that I was nine or ten or twelve years old; I was not. I was four. You see, I have a condition that allows me to remember most days of my life since I was two years old.

For years, I just thought that I had a great memory until I saw a television special that featured people with this same ability. This ability is called hyperthymesia and can be a blessing or a curse. There are many different levels of it, and mine is not as dramatic as some others. I never know when it will hit. I can be fine and going about my day, and out of the blue, my mind will take me to a place in 1971 or 1980. All of a sudden, I can tell you more about what I did in 1974 than what I did last week.

When it starts, I can close my eyes and mentally and physically put myself in that day. I hear the sounds, smell the smells, and feel the happiness and pain as vividly as I did that day. I lose sense of my current state, and as long as I am not startled, I can be in that time for a long while.

The great thing about it is I can go back to happy

times and be with past family and friends who are long since gone. The downside is that I also go back to bad times, very bad times, and relive all of the pain that occurred on a specific day. I never know where my mind will carry me.

It's hard to live in the present, when your mind leads you back. It is something that God has given me for a reason, and I will have it till I die, I suppose. I try to stay very busy and not let my mind wander much, but it isn't something you have a lot of control over.

While life was great, things were about to change, and I mean change dramatically. My mother was meeting many different people in her new career, and my dad was stuck in his mundane, regular-man's job in Atlanta. Once again, the newness wore off the lake house move, and they started arguing and fighting all of the time. I remember that the arguing would make me physically sick and nervous. I used to hide under my bed and in my closet with my childhood companion (my extra-large-size Winnie the Pooh). I would hide and pray for God to make them quit arguing.

After a while, I guess they got sick of each other and wanted to get a divorce. This was the day that everything in my life changed. My mother kicked my dad out, and we were alone – just my mother, my brother, and me. It was over, no more arguing and fighting, but no more family. My dad moved back home to his parents' house. We made our way for a while, and I was trying to come to terms with what happened to my happy life. I remember thinking and hoping this was a temporary situation and that they would get back together. Little did I know that it would be the last time I would see my parents in the same room together until my grandmother and aunt died thirty-seven years later.

CHAPTER 2

The End of My Parents' Marriage

———— ⌒ ————

R ight after they were divorced, I continued to go to my grandmother's house daily, and I got to see my dad frequently. We continued living at the lake house, and shortly thereafter my mother began seeing an older man who seemed to have a lot of money. This new relationship was a shock for me and my brother as it killed us to see our mother with another man, especially so soon after the divorce.

I wasn't quite five years old, all of my security and peace were gone, and I now had to deal with a new man. *No thanks, bring my daddy back*, I thought. This new man didn't last very long, and he was no longer coming around. *Whew, I'm glad he's gone.* Much later in life, several people told me that my mother left my dad for this man, but it didn't work out for her.

My parents had a terrible, bitter divorce. She said

my dad was mentally abusive to her and even hit her one time. He claimed she cheated on him and was mentally abusive to him. So, all of my life neither of my parents would assume any personal responsibility for their actions. Now, as a successful, married adult with children of my own, it amazes me how quickly they gave up and threw everything away. They should have had counseling or tried harder to make their marriage work. Looking back now, my dad didn't want the divorce. My mother was the one who wanted out.

After the divorce, I spent many nights at my grandmother's and my two aunts' houses while my mother was out trying to advance her career. I can remember my uncle telling her she needed to be a mother to her children and she needed to stay home with them more. I loved going to my aunts' houses when I was a child because I felt a security and was reminded of how my life used to be. To this day, I am very close to my grandmother and my aunts because they were so good to me when I was a child. It was almost like I could be part of a normal family in place of my own because mine was far from normal. This was a pattern for me most of my life – trying to fit in with or be a part of other people's lives, people who had normal families. I put too much emphasis on other personal relationships – trying to fill the void in my life.

After my mother's relationship was over, she struggled along in her new career, and my dad paid child support. Once again, my mother met another man at another party. He was forced into our lives in swift fashion. I knew the first time I laid eyes on him that I didn't like him. He was a divorced, military doctor/medic, who worked at South Fulton Hospital and was in the National Guard. I can remember being four years old and crying, telling my mama that I was scared of him and that I didn't like that "old beardy man." He actually had a mustache, but as a small child, everyone with a beard or mustache was a "beardy man." He lived in an apartment in East Point, and he wined and dined my mom. Once again, I didn't want any part of this new man. I wanted my mama and daddy to get back together, but of course this would never happen.

I can remember every Christmas of my childhood after my parents' divorce. When I sat on Santa's lap, he would ask what I wanted for Christmas, and I would ask for an Evel Knievel stunt bike and a skateboard or a go-cart like every other kid. Then, every year, I would whisper in his ear and ask him if he could make my mama and daddy get back together. I look back now and wonder what Santa thought with my gift request.

Everything moves fast when you are five years old and coping with a new and dysfunctional life. My mother and her new man were married, unannounced to anyone, and there we were. We had a new stepdad without my mother asking or talking to us about how we felt or what we thought. It's like we didn't matter anymore.

This marriage and the lack of concern for what my brother and I thought would be a source of turmoil in my relationship with my mother for many, many years. I wanted to ask her: *You were my mother, why were you so selfish? Why didn't you ask us? Why didn't you care what we thought?* From that day on, I never had any respect or trust in my mother. This was a difficult way to grow up and led to a hard way as an adult. For years I struggled with my faith in God because I couldn't trust or have faith and security in my earthly parents. How, then, could I trust my heavenly Father?

This was a problem I struggled with for many years

until our pastor, Charles Stanley, explained that no matter how badly our earthly parents have behaved, we have a loving heavenly Father who will never leave us or forsake us. The day I learned that was one of the most pivotal days on my life. I had never thought of God that way. God had always been a taskmaster to me, someone who kept me under his thumb and didn't want me to be too happy. God was someone whom I cried out to as a child, but he never came to rescue me. Dr. Stanley and Isaiah 41:10 cleared that right up for me.

After my mother remarried, we moved to East Point. No more family, no more going to my grandmother's house every day, no more seeing my dad weekly, no more family roots. We lived in East Point about two years, and I attended kindergarten and first grade in a strange place with unfamiliar people. I've never told anybody this, but I felt like I had been abducted by strangers and held against my will for many years. I was trapped in a life I didn't want and could do nothing about. This new chapter in my young life would set the course of discouragement and my lack of security for years to come.

My mother carried on with her real-estate career

in East Point, and my brother and I once again were trying to adjust to another major life change. I was now five years old, and he was nine. My brother has always been my faithful stalwart, and we are close to this day. I think it's because we were in the trenches together for so many years when we were little. Because my brother was four years older than me, the divorce was much harder him.

To this day, I can't believe that my mother never got any counseling for my brother or me. My mother had always been good about burying her head in the sand and making herself believe that things weren't as bad as they seemed. They weren't for her, but life was miserable for my brother and me. I love my mother; she gave me life, and she is good to me, my children, and my wife, but for many years, I felt she had been self-centered and put her needs and those of her current husband before her own children.

CHAPTER 3

The Bad Years

————⁓————

Now, back to what I refer to as the "bad years." Once we moved to East Point, my brother and I quickly realized how bad this was going to be. Everything was like the military. We were turned into a couple of five- and nine-year-old slaves. At this early age, we were expected to dust, vacuum, wash dishes, clean bathrooms, work in the yard, iron his military uniforms, wash the cars, and tend to whatever dog they bought. As bad as all the work was, the mental abuse shortly followed, along with the physical abuse and the constant threat of physical abuse, and I was a mere five years old.

I can remember the first time our stepfather ever took his anger out on me. I was five and trying to survive with this new tyrant. We had some ducks in a cage out in the back yard that my brother and I had to maintain. This guy hated these ducks because our dad had bought them for us at Easter.

One day, he sent me out to clean the cages. There were swarms of bees around the cages, and I was scared. I kept trying to be brave; it was either get stung or get in trouble. I kept trying, but I just couldn't do it. So I went to hide. He came looking for me when he realized the cages weren't cleaned.

He dragged me across the yard and threw me screaming into the bees and the cages. I quickly got up and ran because earlier that year before moving to East Point, I had been stung in the mouth by a bumble bee and had to go to the doctor. I was terrified of bees.

I ran in the house to hide from my new stepdad, who was hunting me. He was screaming and yelling and trying his best to find me. I could hear him slamming doors and turning things over as he looked for me. He finally found me.

I remember the rage in his eyes. He dragged me into the carport, where he beat me with a metal welding rod. I thought I was going to die. Blood ran down into my shoes. *Where was my mother? Where was my dad? Where was God*, I remember thinking.

When my mother put me in the tub that night, she saw my legs and asked me how this had happened. I told her, and I begged her not to tell him because I knew he acted totally different when she was not home. She confronted him and told him not to ever touch her children again or she would leave him. Did this happen? No. The minute she left the bathroom, he came and gave me an evil look and said, "I will get you for this. I will make it so you don't ever get to go see your daddy and Nannie ever again."

This event set the pattern for my life with this person for the next eight years. I don't think I had a good night's sleep in their house from that day forward. I had a perfectly good bedroom, but I was deathly afraid to sleep alone, for I really thought he would kill me. So I slept with my brother in the bed next to the wall for most of my childhood years.

The next day everything was back to normal in what I used to call "Mama's world." I went to kindergarten, my brother went to school, the tyrant did whatever it was that he did every day, and Mama went to her real estate office. I was dreading and afraid to go home, for I knew what was going to happen. He didn't beat me that day, but what he said to me haunts me to this day. How a grown man could talk to a five-year-old kid that way amazes me. God says that the wicked will be punished. I'd say, wherever this guy is now, I hope God is working on him.

I quickly realized that this man was nuts, and my mother was not going to leave him. She should have left him after the first beating, but she didn't. By this point, I was five, almost six years old and knew that if my brother and I were going to survive, we had better learn to wear two hats if you will, one where we would be nice and avoid the abuse and the second where we figured out how we would ever get out of this terrible life.

This man was clever. He would suck up and be so nice to my mother and to us while she was home and then become a monster when she was gone. I used to call my mother every day and ask when she was coming home, hoping she would get there before he did. Looking back now, she had to know how bad we hated this guy and how he treated us, but she never did anything about it. This man knew he had so much leverage and fear over us that we didn't dare mention a word about anything to my mother. Maybe, in her mind, since she didn't hear about it, nothing was wrong.

One of our stepdad's favorite tactics when we would threaten to tell on him for whatever he had done to us was to say, "I will fix it to where you will never be able to see your daddy or grandparents anymore." This was a powerful, intimidation tool on five and nine year-old children. You see, back in the early seventies, divorce judges always gave full custody to the mother. This meant that if we behaved and kept our mouths shut, we got to see our dad, our grandparents and our home-town, one weekend a month. I lived this way from the time I was five until I was almost fourteen years old.

After living in East Point for two years or so, they decided we needed to build a new house, and we moved out to Douglasville. Okay – something new, a fresh start, we thought maybe this guy would treat us better. Wrong. There were short spells of normalcy, followed by bad times that would last for weeks. I don't know if he was bi-polar or just unstable.

By the time we moved into the Douglasville house, I had learned to ride a bicycle. This was my greatest escape. The neighborhood we moved into was a classic seventies neighborhood. All the houses were new, and there were lots of kids to play with. It was a place and a time in the world where you could turn your kids loose, and they would be okay.

Shortly after the novelty of the new house wore off, the abuse returned with a vengeance. I was then and have always been a survivor so I tried to adapt to the situation. It was a tough deal for an eight-year-old as I juggled all the life problems I had. I learned to stay busy and was gone as much as I could be. I played every sport and learned as many things as I could. As soon as I would get home from school, I would hurry to get my work done so I could get on my bike or skateboard and leave. I used to hate suppertime and dark because that meant I had to go home.

The memories of the times I spent with my childhood friends who had normal families are priceless. These folks, along with times I spent at my aunts' houses, gave me hope and taught me what kind of life I wanted to have someday. Basically, I learned from my own parents what NOT to do and everything else from the rest of my close family and from my friends' families. Most people get their foundation and life lessons from their own parents. I can honestly say that I received no positive life lessons from my parents; I did, however, learn what NOT to do. I guess that's why I have devoted my life to being the best parent I can be to my own children.

CHAPTER 4

The Sunday Afternoon Kids

⎯⎯⎯⎯⎯ ∽ ⎯⎯⎯⎯⎯

After moving to Douglasville, I was beginning to understand the adult manipulation and mind games. One day when I was ten, I was getting thrashed because he figured out I was hounding my mother about when she was going to come home every day. I remember thinking, *Thanks a lot, Mama. By telling on me, you are the reason I am getting this; you are just like him.* That was the day I decided I had had enough of the abuse. I told him after the attack when my adrenaline was flowing that I would kill him someday – and to sleep tight. He looked at me kind of shocked and then chased me out of the house. After that day, he never laid another hand on me. The intense mental abuse and intimidation, however, continued for years. I harbored resentment towards my mother that at our young ages, my brother and I had to face these situations.

During all of these years, we were allowed to go see

our dad one weekend a month. Those visits were our reason for living. As adults, most people know what it's like to count down days on your calendar to your vacation or some other important date. We grew up counting down the days to when we could go see our dad and be home. I used to get so excited on the Friday of our departure that I could hardly make it through the school day. It was the greatest feeling in the world on those Fridays, followed by the worst feeling in the world on Sunday afternoons when it was time to go back.

I remember crying in the car when my dad had to carry us back. To this day, I get an uneasy feeling from three to four o'clock on Sunday afternoons. It was this kind of constant emotional roller coaster that happened every month of my growing-up years.

I get so tired of divorced people who say how well their kids are doing. My message for them is –You keep thinking that for your own sake, but realize this: Your children and your grandchildren's lives will never be as they should be. Don't be so selfish. Work out your differences with your spouse. If not, at least get your kids some counseling and get them into church.

There is a convenience store up the road from where

we have lived and raised our own children for the last twenty-one years. Many Sunday afternoons you can see people bringing their kids back from one spouse to be returned to the other after their weekend visits, just like I had to do. There is one little guy I've seen a couple of times who is always crying and upset when he is getting out of the car carrying his suitcase. He looks about six or seven years old. His parents don't speak or interact when the kids are switching cars. It appears as though they have both remarried; the new husband handles the swap, and the wife sits in the car. This little guy was really upset the last time I saw them. I saw his stepdad giving him that evil eye while telling him to dry that mess up and being verbally abusive to him. Of course, this was after his real dad had pulled away. My heart ached for that little guy, and how I so badly wanted to help that child.

I wanted to confront his stepdad, but God restrained me and spoke to my heart saying, *Finish your book, do it for all the little children.* I think of this family and those poor children as I write. That little guy was me when I was that age. *How many kids across America go through this Sunday afternoon turmoil each week,*

I thought. That little guy, with tears running down his face and clutching his small suitcase, inspired me to create my foundation: *The Sunday Afternoon Kids*. This foundation will offer free counseling and help to children and parents before, during, and after a divorce.

During the next few years, a strange thing was happening. My brother and I were growing up, and we weren't going to be living in this turmoil much longer. By this time, my mother and this guy were arguing and fighting all the time – sounds familiar, doesn't it? I discovered a strange thing: When my mother and dad would argue, I was sick to my stomach and felt like I could die, but when she argued with her second husband, it made me happy. I was happy because they were getting what they deserved. It also meant that they might split up. One could only hope. They both had been divorced before; maybe it could happen again – maybe. For years, I covertly did everything I could to cause them to argue.

CHAPTER 5

Mr. Ralph

———— ∽ ————

When I was twelve or thirteen years old and going on thirty-five, I had already gone through more stress and heartache than most people three to four times my age. One of the ways I coped was to learn whatever I could about fishing and cars. I read everything I could get my hands on and watched every television show that I could. Fishing and cars were like sports for me, another escape from reality. I fished every chance I got. I would fish in lakes, creeks, or every time we went to the ocean.

The father of one of my friends up the street knew how much I loved to fish, and he would take us often. Mr. Ralph and his family were the first people to introduce me to Jesus. They were good people and genuinely cared about me and my salvation. Mr. Ralph taught me how to tie my first fishing knots. He would take us kids over to Treasure Lake in the next county in their lime green Vista Cruiser. We caught bass, catfish, and bream. He mentored us and talked to us about God and life.

I can remember it was strange for me to hear people talk so openly about God. Their family was inspirational in my going to Christian school in the sixth, seventh, and eighth grades. I enjoyed being around their family as they were normal, and they cared about their children.

Also, during these years, my Nannie Samples would come spend the weekend a few times a year, and it was an escape from the reality of my existence. I always hated it when we had to take her home because she lived back in our old hometown. It was torture to go back home and not be able to stay. I remember one time we saw my dad's car in town when we were taking Nannie home. I wanted so badly to jump out of the car and run, but I couldn't. I remember the size of the lump I had in my throat and being so upset, but I knew I couldn't show any emotion because my stepdad would lower the boom on me if my mother thought anything was wrong.

He kept us on a tight leash, hiding from my mother

that anything was wrong or anything that would disrupt their lives. At this point, I had had enough, and it was time to take control of my own life. Since the time he was fourteen years old, my brother was telling me that the only reason he stayed there was because of me. At that time in Georgia, the law said that when you reached fourteen years of age, you could appear before a judge and tell him which parent you wanted to live with. Since I was thirteen, we wouldn't have too much more time to wait before we could go live with my dad.

As time went on, my mother and stepdad's fights got worse and worse. I used to enjoy it when they fought and argued; now I was getting really tired of it. Also, I started noticing how quickly their arguments became volatile. Something had happened, something was different, and I couldn't figure out what had changed.

One day I was playing basketball in the driveway, and my mother came outside. He followed her out, and they began to argue. He said, "Your children should know what you have done." I knew this was heading in a very bad direction. He said again, "if you don't tell him, I will." She threatened him to keep his mouth shut, but he paid her no mind. He accused her of some terrible things and they argued badly. I can remember I wasn't shocked; I was just numb to the whole ordeal. It was par for the course for our lives. Nothing surprised me anymore.

How could I be involved with such loser people and have such a loser family? How could this be my family? I spent most of life being embarrassed about my family and ashamed of the first part of my life. I had nothing to do with it, but I felt these people were a reflection on me. I spent most of my life trying to make up for and compensate for my parents' bad choices and our bad lives.

This made me an over-achiever in everything I've ever done. I had to do everything I could to make up for and to be better than my family legacy. I over-compensated on many things as I tried to be the polar opposite of my family. Many children and adults of childhood divorce spend their entire lives trying to make up for the mistakes of their parents. These children feel ashamed, insecure, and many will feel "less than," no matter how much they achieve in life. It is common for these children to think people with normal families and normal childhoods are somehow better than they are. They feel like others are better qualified because they grew up secure with a strong family foundation. I felt this way for many years; after all, I had grown up with none of this.

After their big altercation in the driveway, their relationship was up and down for a while. I remember being angry with my mother because she was doing everything she could to work it out with this loser, but she didn't try to work out anything with my dad.

One of the problems with my stepdad was that he was a borderline alcoholic. They were always going here or there to a party, or having a party. He drank beer at home like it was going out of style. Alcohol eventually would be their downfall. What you are about to read, I have never told anyone, verbally or in writing, until now.

CHAPTER 6

Not a Normal Sunday

———— ⌁ ————

It all started one Sunday morning. It was a normal weekend in our neighborhood – people were cutting their grass, getting ready for church, and I remember it was hot. I had asked my mom and stepdad to take me fishing at a lake located about twenty minutes from our house and one I had never fished before. I was amazed that they agreed to take me. They even planned a day around it.

We got our stuff together and brought our lunch; they brought a cooler full of beer. My mother tanned in the sun, and we fished. Everything seemed okay, especially since the events of the prior week. I remember catching some really big bream that day and trying to enjoy a few moments of peace. As the day wore on, he drank more and more, and out of the blue, another major argument started.

Here we go again, I thought. So we had to pack up

our stuff all in a mutter and start home. As many of my days were with these two people, another decent day was ruined by drinking and arguing. My stepdad was obviously drunk and belligerent and was remembering the argument they had the day before. He insisted on driving home and was in no shape to do so. He refused to let her drive, and he won the battle. They argued violently the whole way home.

Some things children don't need to hear, and I heard a lot of terrible things that day, as I had many times in my young life. Once we got home, the argument was to the point of violence, and they finally went about their business for about an hour. It was almost sundown, and my brother and I had just finished our once-a-week phone conversation with our daddy. We were allowed fifteen to twenty minutes maximum when they were feeling generous. It was a long-distance call, and they didn't want a high phone bill. I think it was more of a control thing because they knew we were never happy once we got off the phone with him or came back from visiting him.

No, we weren't happy – we missed our daddy and our hometown where life was normal, a place where we were supposed to be, and our parents should have been together. But no, we were basically held against our wills in a terrible situation. Years later, I think my mother still lives in denial. I think that's how she copes with the mistakes in her life. She says those were great days for her – some of the best days of her life. I find that to be very disturbing since they were among the worst days of our lives.

CHAPTER 7

Our Night of Terror

———— ∽ ————

We finished up on the phone with our daddy and went to our rooms. It was a school night as I remember, and things were winding down. The TV show *60 Minutes* was coming on. (To this day, the sound of that clock ticking on television makes me feel sick.) I was looking out the window and wishing for a better life when all of the sudden, I heard a loud crash. My mother had locked my stepdad out of the house, and he had smashed in the glass door. Glass flew everywhere. He attacked my mother, hitting her violently, and she collapsed to the floor. I thought he had killed her, and I just knew that we were next.

Even though my mother had betrayed me for many years and in many ways, my instinct was to defend her, my brother, and myself. He started down the hall in my direction, and I quickly ducked back into my brother's bedroom. My stepdad saw me; he knew that I had seen him batter my mother. He said in a loud voice, "You are next."

I still had my fish cleaning knife on my belt, and I reached for it. I was not afraid anymore. My adrenaline was flowing, and I was going to defend us. He saw me reach for my fish knife and said with that evil look, "Let me get my knife out." So he reached in his pocket and got out his knife. He kept coming towards me, all the while saying, "Come on . . . Come on."

By this time, my mother was back on her feet and saw him coming down the hall at me. She tried to intervene, but he shoved her out of the way. We were in close hand-to-hand combat, and all I could see was the shining blade on his knife. My brother was behind me swinging a club at my stepdad but missing him. I thought to myself, *I will not die today.* So with all the strength my thirteen-year-old body could muster, the eight years of mental and physical abuse that was all bottled up inside me came out, and I defended my life and the lives of my brother and my mother.

Our attacker fell back into the hall and disengaged.

(I would never recommend violence in any way – only in a life-threatening situation when self-defense is the only way to survive.) It was not a good scene. My mother screamed for us to get to the car.

Looking back now, my memory of that night is in slow motion, but in real time, these events happened quickly. She yelled again, "get to the car." I had about two seconds to grab something and leave. I figured we were leaving for good and never coming back, so the only thing I grabbed was my old trusty childhood companion – my Winnie the Pooh.

With my Pooh and my knife, I ran out to the car. The car would not crank. We got out and ran to the second car, and it would not crank either. This seemed strange because both vehicles were running perfectly earlier that day. Later we found out that he had disabled both vehicles before the altercation so we would not be able to leave.

After we discovered this, the reality of what could have happened that day set in. We could have all been killed. This man had these events pre-planned. He had pre-meditated his actions by disabling the vehicles before he smashed in the door, attacked my mother, and was going to attack us.

Looking back now, I really believe that God protected me that day. He protected my mother and my brother as well. For years, I would not share this information with anyone; I carried it around like a cumbersome suitcase. I was glad that I did what I did to protect my life and my family's, but I felt embarrassed, ashamed, and angry with my mother for putting me in this terrible position – I was a thirteen-year-old child. I didn't deserve these events or the life that she had thrust upon me. What divorced mothers and fathers don't realize or even think about is that even though their children seem okay or well adjusted, they will carry the scars of their childhood to their graves.

When we realized neither car would start, we set out on foot. It was getting dark, but that didn't seem to matter. My mother had a real-estate office a few miles away as the crow flies. So we headed in that direction. It seemed like we walked for hours. Up and down hills, from one subdivision to another and through another.

We finally made it to the busy highway and walked about a quarter mile to get there.

I wonder what the people in their cars were thinking, seeing a bruised woman and two kids, one with a Pooh bear, walking up the side of the road after dark. Nobody stopped to help us or offer us a ride, but that didn't seem to matter. We made it to the real-estate office and got inside. My mother called the police to tell them what happened.

During this time, our attacker made his way to a phone and called his German friend down the street. This man called an ambulance and the police. He was transported to the hospital and went into surgery. He stayed in the hospital for about a week and never returned to our home. I was questioned by the police that night, and while scared to death, I told them I was defending my life, as well as my mother's and my brother's. I told the officer about the years of mental and physical abuse, and the cop actually said, "He's lucky you didn't kill him." The nice officer gave me his card and said if he ever showed any signs of aggression toward me again, to call him or the sheriff's office. The officer took my knife for evidence and left the real-estate office.

My mother came up with a car for us, but we were afraid to go home. She took us down to the house of a male friend of hers about an hour away. I asked her where we were going, but she would not say. It was the middle of the night, and I couldn't understand where we were going, driving out into the countryside. It seemed much longer than the hour it took, but we finally arrived at a farm, way out in the middle of nowhere.

When we got out, the man was kind and friendly. I didn't feel afraid of him. I had no idea who he was, but I remember thinking he must have been a business associate from her work.

Looking back now, how she knew this man was not important. This was probably the best decision she had ever made as this man would eventually wind up being my second stepdad and her third husband. He is truly a hardworking, kind, fair, and decent man. I only wish she would have met him before the abusive tyrant we had just spent eight years with. My mother and her third husband have been successfully married for over thirty years. I guess the third time is the charm.

Anyway, we spent the night and most of the next day out in the country and then returned home. It was a confusing, scary time for a thirteen-year-old. I was angry with my mother, and I felt as though I couldn't trust her or believe a word she said.

CHAPTER 8

Fishing For Therapy

———— ⌣ ————

W hen we arrived back home, I couldn't look at
the place the same ever again. My mother
worked to get the blood off the floor and walls. We
cleaned up the glass from the smashed storm door.
I remember thinking, *How are we going to live here*?
Our once-friendly neighbors would only stare at us
and go inside their houses. All of my neighborhood
friends weren't allowed to play with me. This was very
hard on me as I had done nothing wrong. These people
didn't know the whole story, and I would never get to
tell them until now.

After taking a few days off, I returned to my seventh-
grade classroom at my Christian school. At this point,
many of the kids at school who had been my friends
would have nothing to do with me because they had
heard what happened. I was on the football team, and
my teammates would barely speak to me anymore. It
was a very hard time in my life. I was being rejected by
people who only the week before were my close friends.
My teacher even treated me differently.

It became so difficult that I could no longer stand the bad treatment. So after my mother left for work, my brother and I would go hide at the river all day, and I would fish. Fishing gave me peace. When I fished, I could pray and escape from my life. I remember praying most of my young life, *God, why is this happening to me? Why won't you help me? Why won't you save me from this terrible life? If you loved me, God, you wouldn't have let all of this happen to me.* These were questions I would struggle with for the next thirty years.

So I would fish, and we would go home before my mother arrived home from work, and she never knew we didn't go to school that day. This lasted for a couple of weeks until the school called because we had exceeded the limit of allowed absences. When she found out, she was mad at us, but I didn't care. She had destroyed my life, and I had no interest in her opinions. I was kind of like, *Why do you care now? Where have you been for the last eight years?* During the month since the altercation with her second husband, he was showing up at places where we were at. He wouldn't stop, but he would drive through and stare. It was like he was stalking us. It became bad enough that I couldn't ride my bike through the neighborhood because I was afraid he would try to abduct or kill me.

CHAPTER 9

Running Away

————— ∽ —————

At this point in time, I had not been able to play with any of my friends for the past month, and I was alone. I had heard rumors that my mother and her second husband had been talking again and that he might be coming back. My panicked thought was, *Oh my God, how could this be happening?* I couldn't believe a word my mother said so I believed what I had heard from a girl down the street. This girl was the daughter of one of my stepdad's friends. Having heard this, I was in shock, and I was not going to live in that nightmare again. I told my brother, and we hatched a plan.

We collected all the money we could scrounge up between us and decided we were going to run away before this terrible man and my mother got back together. So we got up enough money, and we were going to run away and go live with my dad, who lived in our original hometown two hours away. It took us a few days to get our plan together and assemble what we didn't want to leave behind.

I remember it was a tough thing trying to figure out what I could give up and never see again. It was almost like people preparing for a hurricane or a flood and deciding what to bring and what to leave. It was funny – I was thirteen years old but felt as though I was going on thirty-five. I had dealt with so many adult situations in my young life, but I was only thirteen – still a child – and was really sad about leaving some of my toys and my bicycle behind.

We had to be careful in putting these plans together as we didn't want to alert my mother that we were up to something. It was almost the weekend, and my grandmother was coming to spend it with us. She didn't know that anything had happened, and my mother swore us to secrecy.

I loved when Nannie came to stay with us because it made me feel normal for a short while. This time when she came, my stepdad was gone and we had a great weekend with Nannie. Her visits to our house were always fun. We would go to the mall and Varsity or to a cafeteria and eat lunch. Nannie was a saint and our family patriarch. How she raised a person who such poor judgment as my mother still amazes me. Nannie's other daughters grew up the same way as my mother did. They had a wonderful childhood with their mom and dad and a normal family unit. Both of my mother's sisters, however, are now successful godly women who have kept their families together and prospered. My aunts have always loved me like one of their own. The only security I had during my early life was from Nannie, Aunt Martha and Aunt Hilda.

Even now, I get tired of hearing my mother talk about how great a childhood she had. I think to myself, *Must have been nice to have that – What happened to ours?*

My mother had left to take Nannie back home, which was two hours away, and it was time to put our plan in motion. We had to wait for her to get far enough away so that she would have no chance to come back if they forgot something. So we started to load my brother's car with our stuff. We brought as many of our favorite things as we could, but most of my treasured belongings wouldn't fit, like my bicycle and many other things.

It was getting late – almost 4:30 on that Sunday afternoon, and we had to leave. We made our last look around and went to the car. We had our hundred dollars, and we were going to leave. We got in the car, but it would not start. That's when the panic button went off. What were we going to do – there was no way we could get the car unloaded, and my mother would be home in a couple of hours. At thirteen, I was pretty sharp about cars, and I quickly went into diagnosis mode. The starter was clicking, so I knew the battery was dead, or the starter was messed up. I remembered the headlights came on but were dim, and the car would not crank. I remembered what I had learned from reading about how to crank your car with a screwdriver. So we unpacked our tool box for the road, and I got out a flathead screwdriver and jumped across the solenoid.

That didn't work because the battery was too weak. Now what? We didn't have another car there to jump it off, and we couldn't find the jumper cables. Time was wasting, and we needed to leave. Then I thought, *I will call our old friend up the street, Mr. Ralph, and see if he could help us.*

He was a kind soul and came right away. He brought his jumper cables and jumped us off. We were ready to go. He asked me, "What are ya'll doing? Your car is all packed up." I did not want to lie to him, so I told him the truth.

"We are going to live with my dad," I said. He shook our hands and told us to be careful. He asked if we were ever coming back, and we said, "No sir." He told us again to be careful, and he hoped to see us again someday. I never got to see my old friend again, and recently found out that he had passed. I miss him and his family dearly, and I have never heard from any of them again.

So we drove away. It was not a tearful goodbye for our home, but instead a liberation. We had an additional problem, and it was a big one. There was only one way to our old home town, and mother was coming back from there. What if she saw our car and saw us on the road? We would be caught, and she would know where we were going and what we were doing.

We decided to go the other direction and drive out Hwy. 20 towards Alabama. We would wait till we thought the coast was clear to proceed to my dad's house. What we didn't realize was that it was getting dark, and we were farther from Alabama than we thought. We finally made it to the state line.

It was getting late, so we thought we'd get a motel, but we couldn't because I was thirteen, and my brother was only seventeen. No one would give us a room because we were minors from another state. They would call the police and our mother, and we would be carried back. We were really tired. We saw a sign that said, "Campground next exit." *Oh boy,* we thought, *this might work.*

We got off the interstate and pulled in. It was a mom-and-pop place where the old couple lived behind the office, and we woke them up when we pulled in. They wanted to know how old we were and why we were out so late. We told them we were going home and needed somewhere to rest before continuing on. They were nice and let us in the campground for five dollars. We were paranoid that they were going to call the police, but we were tired and needed to sleep.

That was one of the longest nights of my life, trying to sleep in a car packed full and waking up every time I heard a car go by. Daylight finally came, and I was amazed at what I saw – a lake and a huge set of swings like you would see in a park. Being a child of thirteen, the urge to jump on the swing was just too strong.

My brother told me to get back in the car, but I paid him no mind. I swung as far and as high as I could. So high, I could close my eyes and forget where I was and what I was facing. I then saw a big fish swirl next to the bank. I dug out my fishing rod. My tackle box was buried in the trunk, so I could only use a piece of bread from my bologna sandwich that I had packed the day before. I remember being angry that the fish would not eat my bread, and I could not get to my fishing lures.

About that time, the old couple saw us still there and called the police. The officer was a nice man and asked us a bunch of questions. I thought, *we've been caught,* and I was sure my mother had reported us missing. We explained to him that we were going home and stopped to rest. He seemed okay with that and left. Wow! *He didn't make us go with him*, we thought.

We got in the car and left. Having spoken with the police, we thought that if we went back into Georgia through our original county, we would be spotted by their police and picked up. Once again I adjusted the plan. I came up with the idea that we would go to Birmingham, Alabama, head north, and then back east into Georgia. We hadn't planned on a different route to our hometown, and we didn't have a map.

We made it to Birmingham and stopped at a McDonalds drive-thru. It was great to eat and have a coke. We proceeded north in heavy afternoon traffic, and all of a sudden, WHAM… We were rear-ended. We got out to look at our bumper – it was dented, The other car was messed up as well. We told the driver we were fine and didn't care about the dent. "Let's just forget it," we said and keep the traffic moving. What we really meant was – we don't need the police coming out and getting our information.

We headed north in Alabama, and it was getting dark again. Needless to say, we got lost. The road signs in Alabama in those days were not great. They were difficult to read at night, and there was nowhere to get a map. So we drove and guessed which direction to go. We were one hundred percent lost out in the country and did not know that we were about to cross the state line. Yes, back in Georgia. Lost, but back in Georgia.

I knew we had to continue east the best way we could and keep moving. Seemed like we drove forever, but out of the blue I saw a sign that said "Rome Speedway." Oh my Lord, it was one of my aunt and uncle's race tracks. God had led us to a familiar spot.

The only problem was, the track was closed, and they lived two hours away. I had been to that track with them many times as a kid but didn't know how to get there. So, we kept driving, and while not as lost as earlier, we still had no idea which way to go. We drove and drove down country roads, and it was very dark. Something told me we needed to turn left. We did and Hallelujah! We came upon something familiar; I was shocked and amazed that we were on Hwy. 369 headed toward our childhood home.

Looking back thirty years later, I now realize that the "something" was God. He was directing us in the darkness. We were scared and alone and didn't know which way to turn, and he was there taking care of us, leading us home. It makes me emotional to think back now and realize that God was taking care of us then, even though I didn't know it at the time. He had always been taking care of me. There is no other explanation as to how we drove down so many roads through Alabama without a map and in the dark. There is no doubt that God led us home.

I think back to these miracles in my life and wonder, *why have I ever doubted God and his presence in my life?* I have wasted a lot of years wondering why God would have allowed me to suffer and endure such hardship. I now realize he was molding me into who I am today. He was shaping my life to where I could someday help parents who are considering divorce and other children who are struggling to cope with divorce. I want to tell them that they are not alone. God loves them and has a plan for their lives, a plan to prosper them and give them great joy and hope. I want to tell them to keep praying and keep living one day at a time.

Once we turned onto Hwy. 369, we were only twenty minutes from home. We were actually going to make it. We stopped at a store and called my dad to tell him we were coming to his house. He said everyone was worried about us. Apparently, the night before, my mother had realized we were gone, and she called my grandmother, who called everyone in the family. It's strange; we were gone for almost two nights, and no one ever called the police. Many years later, I found out my mother had called them after all, and she went looking for us.

Upon driving to my dad's, we decided we didn't want to drive up in the yard. We thought the police or my mother would be there and make us go back. My grandparents lived about a quarter mile from my dad, so we parked behind my grandpa's chicken houses and walked the rest of the way. About midnight, we made it to his driveway. We heard a lady's voice screaming, and she was running towards us in the dark. I thought it was my mother, but it wasn't; it was my dear Aunt Hilda, my mother's sister. She hugged us and was crying and said she thought something bad had happened to us. She had been at my dad's house, waiting by the phone since they heard we were missing.

We went into the house and saw my dad and uncle. I asked them if we were going to have to go back, and they said no; we never had to go back to that awful place. Hallelujah! After nine years of mental and physical abuse, I was free. I was liberated. God had delivered me. I was so tired of it all, so exhausted that I went to sleep. That was one of the best night's sleep of my life.

I felt as though it was all a dream – like being held captive and being freed after all those years

For the next week, we adjusted to our new life with my dad. It was strange being in our hometown and living full time with my dad because for the previous nine years, we only came two days a month. It was all new and fun. We were finally getting to live our dream.

I entered the middle school near our home, and a new chapter had begun. Starting a new school was tough. I remembered everyone from when I was five years old and uprooted from my childhood home, but most of them had forgotten about me. Nine years had passed, and we were now in the eighth grade. I was home where I was supposed to be, where I should have always been, and nobody knew me. It was like starting all over again, except I was like a stranger in my hometown school.

My brother went to high school and experienced the same thing. After a few weeks of living with my dad, reality came crashing down on me. My dad, whom I had spent very little time with since I was four, had no idea how to be a full-time parent and provider. He had been a bachelor for ten years, and when we came up to visit once a month, it was more like a mini vacation for us and him, but he was not accustomed to being responsible for two other people on a daily basis. His place was small compared to the place we had left. His income was adequate to support himself and to pay his child support, but not enough for three people to live on full time.

After my parents had divorced many years before, my dad had not recovered emotionally or financially. My grandparents had given him some land and a place to live. They were great people and did a lot for their children, even when they were adults. Everything was a struggle at my dad's house. Money for clothes, food, and medical care was always an issue. We had no idea that it was going to be this way. We had no idea that he was in such bad shape. After all, we only saw him two days a month for nine years.

School was tough, and my home life was tougher. Once again, I was trapped. No way was I going back to the place I had worked so hard to leave, but staying here was going to be difficult. I hated struggling to get by, and I hated asking my dad for lunch money and clothes money, so at fourteen years old, I got a job. I went to school during the day and worked at a local restaurant washing dishes and doing odd jobs when I could. I would help my grandpa in his chicken houses and pick up hay for a man who had a dairy farm down the road. While my friends were playing sports and having fun, I worked until ten o'clock at night and then went to school the next day.

It was rough, but I was happy to have my own money. I was the only eighth grader I knew who paid for his own school lunch, bought his own clothes, shoes, food, and other necessities. My dad must have been able to make enough for himself and my older brother as my brother didn't work through his senior year or after he got out of high school. He always had clothes, a car, and gas money. I always thought he was my dad's favorite since he was the first-born. I always felt like an outsider.

While I went to school and worked, my brother was able to go to technical school, then four years of college. I had been working to survive and better my own life since I was fourteen. My brother is a great guy. He is very generous to my children, my wife, and me. He has never married or had any children of his own.

When we were kids, he used to tell me that he would never get married, and he never has.

Whenever I could, I would go fishing at Spot Lake or Lake Lanier. When I was fifteen, I took a job at a local auto parts store and also worked at the restaurant. I was going to high school full time and working forty hours a week. I was determined not to be like my dad. I was making more money than my dad was or any of my friends. I didn't get to have much fun or a social life, but that was fine.

Working and having my own money meant freedom. My dad had zero parenting skills, and I have basically been self-supportive since the age of fourteen. I had a place to sleep and do laundry, but that was about it. My children are now fifteen and nineteen, and it makes my heart hurt knowing what I have been through and did at their age just to survive.

At this point in my life, I was saved, but God was missing in my life, or now that I look back, I was missing in his. I harbored a lot of resentment towards my earthly parents and my heavenly Father for allowing me to have such a tough lease on life. As I reflect back,

I realize God was there all the way, even when I didn't know it.

When I was sixteen, I came home from work one day, and my dad started in on me. He was in a rage and accused me of something I had nothing to do with. We argued and he told me to get out. I basically said, "No problem." I packed my stuff and left.

I was now homeless and had nowhere to go in the wintertime. I wasn't going to my relatives, and I was a minor so I could not book a motel room. So I lived in my car for four weeks. It was tough and I was cold and lonely, but I survived. I would go to the laundromat to wash my clothes, and I would shower in the locker room at school.

The mother of one of my friends noticed my laundry basket in my car a couple of times and saw my pillow and blankets. She asked me if I was sleeping in my car, and I said yes. She was upset and invited me to live with them. I stayed with them for six months. It was great to have people who cared about me and had a normal family unit. God sent me the Bolden family at a time when I desperately needed help and guidance.

Mr. Bolden had a heart attack, and I needed to give

them their lives back so after six months, I moved out. I was in the eleventh grade and hadn't spoken to my family in six months. I really had nowhere to go, but God was leading me. I was not going to live in my car again. So I arranged with my brother to ask my dad if I could sleep at his place again – just sleep – and then leave each day. My dad said yes, and we salvaged a strained relationship that was difficult for me for many years.

During this time, I was growing up, accumulating money, and meeting some great people – people who I wanted to be like – good people, successful people, and people with good families. I have never had much respect for people who can't keep their families together or people who don't make a difference for the next generation. During this time of my young life, my mother was not a part of my life. I wanted nothing to do with her. She had caused me a lot of grief and pain over the previous years, and I blamed her for my bad life.

This was a tough time for her as well. Her sisters were angry with her for many years for not taking care of her children and living the life she had been living. I would only speak to my mother maybe once a year over the next ten years. She missed everything in my life from the time I was fourteen till I was twenty-four, due primarily to the fact that I wanted nothing to do with her. Today I'd change some of that if I could, but it's too late.

It was hard on me through my teenage years – not having a mother figure in my life. I basically had no father figure either. While dating, it was tough not to have my mother and father or a suitable home life so I could bring my girlfriend home. Thankfully, I came along at a time when the "car culture" and "cruising" was king. There were no cell phones or pagers. When you wanted to see somebody, you went to town.

By the time I finished high school, I had a new mustang and worked at the parts store forty hours a week. My home life was non-existent so I stayed in town a lot. I would only go home to sleep and do some laundry. There were no loitering laws in our town, and my buddies and I would hang out at night and have fun. Those were great times for me as it all meant an escape from reality.

I remember my altered reality always came down around me on the holidays, when I would be the only one in town on Thanksgiving night and Christmas Eve. Everyone else was home with their families, but not me. I spent many holidays in the shop at the parts store, working on my car all night and listening to the radio.

I had many, many relationships with girls through my teenage years and early twenties, trying to fill the void in my life. It was like trying to live through other people's properly functioning family lives and trying to find one of my own. After graduating high school, many of my friends were going to college and moving on. I didn't have the opportunity to go to college. I was surviving, working, and fishing when I could.

When I was eighteen, I bought my first bass boat. I had some smaller boats when I was twelve through the mid-teens, but the purchase of a bigger boat would change my life because it meant I could spend a lot of time on Lake Lanier, escaping my inner turmoil and honing my craft. At a very young age, I knew my life's calling was fishing, and having a fishing charter business was always my dream.

Being eighteen, I was still very heavily into girls, cars, and having fun. I guess you could say I was slow to grow up, maybe I never will. I had to be an adult at such an early age; I was in no hurry for any responsibility. I bounced from one girl to another; they would get serious, and I would find a way out. I was not ready for a serious commitment.

CHAPTER 10

My Angel

———— ∽ ————

O ne summer God sent my angel to me: my wife,
Pam. I remember the first time I ever saw her
face. My best friend was in love with Pam, and I was
dating someone else. My relationship didn't last, and
Pam and I started hanging out together. Pam was great.
She was pretty, petite and a lot of fun. We were friends
for a while, and then we had our first date.

We dated about two years and had a great thing
going, except for her parents. They were nice folks but
didn't like or approve of our relationship. They didn't
like my background and thought I was unmotivated.
Unmotivated – Me? I was eighteen, had finished school,
and had been working two or three jobs since I was
fourteen. I had a brand new car and a pocket full of
money – but they saw me as unmotivated? Her parents
and I co-existed during the two years of dating, but
they were always difficult and hounded me about college and my future plans. They kept on and on until

finally, I had had enough. I wanted out. I was not going to be judged by folks who knew nothing about me.

I broke up with Pam. She was devastated. It had nothing to do with her, but I was tired of the constant badgering from her parents. I had put up with grief all my young life, and I wanted no part of their hassles anymore. Once again, I was free. Free from responsibility, free from problems. Over the next two years, I lived the life. I had plenty of money, no strings, and I was twenty years old. The days were easy, and the nights were great. My friends were close, and we had a great time. I had several more short relationships during that time, but none seemed to feel right.

After a couple of years, I wanted Pam back and didn't care what her family thought. They were not happy that I was back. They forbade her to see me and said if it continued, she was "free, white and twenty-one" and could move out if she wanted. So she temporarily moved into a friend's apartment.

We continued dating, and I knew we would be together forever. This was hard for me because of the failure of my parents' marriage and the fact that her family strongly disapproved. After a year or so, I got her an apartment of her own and furnished it for her. I bought her a car, and she was settled.

We were married when we were twenty-four. Our marriage was a gift from God. She has been my angel over the last twenty-five years. Her family and I have become closer over the last two decades. They are good people and were only protecting their daughter.

As much as I resisted God's will and tried to fight it, Pam was my destiny. She is one of God's greatest gifts to me, along with Jesus, my children, and my close friends. Over the years, God has done many wonderful things for me. He has protected me, blessed me, saved me, provided for me, counseled me, carried me, and given me all the blessings that I haven't mentioned. Many times I doubted his love and provision in my life. But now, well into my forties, I can see he has been with me every step of the way. I can see his hand in so many areas of my life. The main questions that I get from people all over the world are – *How did you get here?* or *How did you do all of this?* (speaking of my business and achievements). I always say the same thing – it all came from God, I'm just the bait boy. I was simply wandering around, and he led me here.

When I was married and started a family, I reconciled with my mother after many years. It was hard, but it was the right thing to do, and it honored God. I wanted my children to have a normal life in every sense of the word. Over the last twenty years my mother and I have become close again. I forgave her because God forgave me through Jesus. I wasted many years of our lives penalizing her for what she had and had not done for our family. She has changed over the years and is a good grandmother to my children. I am thankful for that.

Since my children were born, my ultimate goal has been to provide a stable, nurturing home life for them. My wife stayed home and raised the children while I built the business. It's been tough at times on one income, but I wanted the best for my sons. I now have one son in college and one son in high school. It is amazing to see how well children with a normal home life and a stable mother and father can thrive and grow as children of God. They both have a strong foundation on which to build their lives. I really believe God allowed me to suffer growing up, in order to build my character to help my children and other families around the world with my story of hope.

CHAPTER 11

My Advice

N̲o matter how bad things seem, always remember, God loves you; he has a will, purpose, and plan for your life. Another question I often get is – who has influenced my life the most. The answer is an easy one: first and foremost my Lord Jesus Christ. I would then say my grandparents, aunts and uncles who kept their families together and prospered. Others who were greatly influential were my early mentor, Jerry Dooley, and our pastor Dr. Charles Stanley. Dr. Stanley has had such a powerful impact on every area of my life. I am thankful for all these people. I would not be here today without them.

With the help of God, I have been able to forgive and deal with the things in my past, but at times I still struggle, especially around Christmas and the holidays. No matter how much you grow or what you may achieve in life, it's a sad reality when your parents are still alive, but not together at Christmas time. For years, I wondered why, why me, why did I get this life, why was I even born? I now realize God was using me for his work and getting me ready to do his big dream in my life. He was simply sanding and polishing me so I could shine for him.

I have dedicated my life to helping children, both young and old, who had divorced parents and terrible childhoods. Please remember, parents, that your children's entire lives will be affected by your decisions. Don't be selfish. Think about your kids. Think about the next generation. You know that doing the right thing by your children is the right thing to do. I pray that God will give you the strength to overcome your differences for the sake of your children.

I've dedicated this book to all the little children in the world, both young and old who need hope for a better day. God can perform miracles – just look at me. Always remember: *Keep Breathing and Keep Believing.* God Loves you. He always has and he always will.

Shane's Life, in Pictures

Shane and Phil Watson

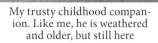

My trusty childhood companion. Like me, he is weathered
and older, but still here

Shane at Nannie's house, almost 2 years old

5 years old and sporting the pirate look

Shane's first media press, 6 years old.
Bicycle Safety Day at school.
(Photo Courtesy Atlanta Journal)

Pitcher for the Mets 5- and 6-yr-old team

Riding my go-kart, while visiting my Dad,
12 years old

18 with my new Mustang

Shane, 5th grade

Deep sea fishing in Destin, 1990

Shane Watson
70" Sailfish
Panama City, Fla.
Boat: Fu-Lin-U-2
October 10, 1988

My first billfish

Shane, 1988

Capt. Shane, 1999 Lake Lanier

Capt. Shane with a nice
Lake Lanier striper

Capt. Shane - A little younger and a little thinner

Capt. Shane, Carolina Skiff photo shoot, 2011

Orange Beach, 2008

Sea Chaser national ad

My favorite billboard that we relocated to the end of the old bait store, 2005

As with everything in my life, this was all God. To all the young folks out there, keep dreaming and keep believing

Shane's beloved Grandmother,
Nannie Samples

Shane's wife Pam, with son
Bradley when he was 11

Shane's wife Pam, with son
Allan when he was 15

Bradley, Pam, Allan, and Shane – PCB 2012

Pam, Allan, Bethany, Bradley, and Shane

About the Author

Over the last thirty years, Shane Watson has become one of the most respected fishing fleet operators in America. He has been featured on television and in print media around the world. His fishing reports and teachings have influenced a generation of people. Shane Watson is a devoted father, husband, mentor, and a member of First Baptist Church of Atlanta. In January 2010, Shane Watson was inducted into "The Freshwater Fishing Hall of Fame" as a Legendary Guide. A statement from the hall of fame reads, *By induction to the Hall, Shane Watson's pioneering spirit will always be remembered.*

Connect with Shane

www.lakelanierstripers.com

Christian Author and Missionary Publishing

Editing, cover design, world-wide distribution, marketing, and everything in between.

We help Christians publish well.